Contents

Chapter 1

What is Fundamentalism?

The Fundamentals

Fundamentalism is a term that can be applied in many areas, but most people use it to describe a set of religious beliefs. Many different religious faiths and denominations are either fundamentalist or have fundamentalist branches. This is true for Christian, Muslim, Jewish, Hindu and other forms of belief.

These branches of fundamentalism are as varied as the religious faiths they spring from, but they have some similarities at their core. The key to this central belief is the word 'fundamental', which describes the real heart of a belief, stripped of unnecessary extras.

Muslim students in northern India learn their lessons at a madrassa, *or religious school. Many Muslim families rely on madrasas to educate their children.*

A health expert might describe the fundamentals of a good diet as a sensible blend of proteins, fruit, vegetables and carbohydrates. Extras such as artificial sweeteners, colouring and preservatives are not necessary and might even be harmful. Religious fundamentalists take a similar view about worship. They believe that the

QUOTE >

'Fundamentalism: A religious movement, which originally became active among various Protestant bodies in the United States after the war of 1914–1918, based on strict adherence to certain tenets (e.g. the literal inerrancy of Scripture) held to be fundamental to the Christian faith. In other religions, especially Islam, a similarly strict adherence to ancient or fundamental doctrines, with no concessions to modern developments in thought or customs.'

Concise Oxford English Dictionary (11th rev. edn), 2006.

FUNDAMENTALISM

Sean Connolly

WAYLAND

First published in 2008 by Wayland

Copyright © Wayland 2008

Wayland
338 Euston Road
London NW1 3BH

Wayland Australia
Level 17/207 Kent Street
Sydney NSW 2000

Senior Editor: Claire Shanahan
Designer: Phipps Design
Photo Researcher: Louise Edgeworth
Proofreader and Indexer: Jo Kemp

British Library Cataloguing in Publication Data
Connolly, Sean, 1956-
Fundamentalism. - (Global issues)
1. Religious fundamentalism - Juvenile literature
I. Title 200.9'04

ISBN 978 0 7502 5432 8

Camera Press, London: p37, Mustafa Hassona p40; Corbis: Bettmann p6,
Gideon Mendel p23, Daniel Brooks p24, Lynsey Addario p32; Getty Images:
Uriel Sinai/Stringer p7, Time & Life Pictures/Stringer p9, Hulton Archive p10,
James Nubile/Image Works/Time & Life Pictures p22, Brennan Linsley/AFP p29;
PA Photos: Channi Anand/AP p4, J. Scott Applewhite/AP p30, Arshia Kiani/AP
p42; Reuters: Amit Dave p5, Bazuki Muhammad p15, Ashikur Rahman p17,
Hamid Mir p18, Erik de Castro p21, Dylan Martinez p26, Atef Hassan p31,
Russell Boyce p34, Carlos Barria p36, Reuters TV/Reuters p38, Mohamed
Azakir p43, Toby Melville p45; Rex Features: Sipa Press p12, Carl Fox p25,
Sipa Press p28, p39.

Printed in China

Wayland is a division of Hachette Children's Books,
an Hachette Livre UK company.
www.hachettelivre.co.uk

Narenda Modi (right), newly elected Chief Minister of the Indian state of Gujarat, waves to supporters after being sworn in on 25 December 2007. Modi is also President of the BJP, a fundamentalist Hindu party.

heart of their belief – its fundamentals can be found in its sacred writings. For Christians, this means the Bible, for Jews it is the Old Testament and later sacred texts, and for Muslims it is the Koran.

Fundamentalists often go much further than simply honouring their sacred books; many of them believe that every word contained in them is absolutely true. Some of these beliefs cannot be proved or even explained through science. A fundamentalist Christian, for example, would believe that the world really was created in six days or that Jesus really did feed 5,000 people with just a few fish and several loaves of bread.

Reaction to the modern world

Fundamentalism seems to flourish when people find themselves threatened or worried by sudden changes going on around them. The 19th century, for example, was a time of rapid scientific and technological advances. New scientific ideas about how old the Earth is and about evolution seemed to contradict some long-held religious beliefs. As a result, some people turned away from religion completely. Others found it possible to retain their faith by viewing sacred texts as being partly symbolic. A third, conservative group came to reject these new theories in favour of a return to the older religious writing.

By 1910, conservative Protestant Christians began using the term 'fundamentals' to describe their essential beliefs. By the 1920s, they became known as 'fundamentalists' and their set of beliefs was called 'fundamentalism'. Over time, the term fundamentalism came to describe any conservative religious belief.

1543 Germans called on to convert or expel all Jews >>>

1881–1884 Pogroms force more than 2 million Jews to flee Russia >>>

1935 Nuremburg Laws strip Jews of their rights and citizenship in Germany >>>

1939–1945 6 million Jews die during the Nazi Holocaust >>>

Black and white

Moral issues are usually black and white for fundamentalists; there is no scope for 'grey areas' or compromise. If a sacred book or tradition says something is so, then many fundamentalists will agree unquestioningly.

Fundamentalists often find themselves in conflict not simply with non-believers, but also with fundamentalists who hold different beliefs. For instance, the Israelis

Civilians and soldiers alike got caught up in the violence of the Thirty Years War, which fuelled Catholic-Protestant conflicts in Europe in the 17th century.

who created new settlements on the West Bank maintain that they are claiming the Bible's Promised Land. The farmers who had lived there until recently are Muslims, whose faith is equally strong.

Fundamentalist Hindus and Sikhs often clash in India about who should be allowed to build a temple on a sacred site. And if there were only one accepted reading of the Bible, there would only be one fundamentalist Christian denomination, instead of the thousands that come to different conclusions after reading the Bible.

Into the spotlight

It can be hard to imagine why – or how – differences of religious opinion have come to feature so much in the modern media. Even as recently as 20 years ago, it seemed that what people believed was a matter for themselves. As long as believers had the freedom to worship, a basic human right in modern society, then no one took much notice of what others believed or how they expressed those beliefs.

Nowadays, it is hard to escape discussions of religion. And it is fundamentalism that has made religion front-page news. In recent years, the media has concentrated on Islamic fundamentalism while spending less time analysing other forms of fundamentalism. That is why this book – with its emphasis on the media – focuses so much on this form of fundamentalism.

The most serious point of fundamentalist conflict centres on relations between Muslim believers and non-believers. The most extreme Muslim fundamentalists believe that the West is an enemy of Islam and must be fought and punished. They look to the Koran and to centuries of Christian-Muslim conflict to justify their views.

732 Charles Martel halts Islam's advance on Europe at the Battle of Tours >>>	**1095–1270** European nations launch Crusades against Muslims in the Holy Land >>>	**1492** Last Muslims driven out of Spain >>>

An Orthodox (fundamentalist) Jew stands on an Israeli tank on the Lebanese border in July 2006. Orthodox Jews often influence Israeli actions.

Peace on Earth?

Fundamentalists sometimes ignore core messages of peace and concentrate instead on their differences with members of other faiths. Christians, whether fundamentalist or not, celebrate the message of 'Peace on Earth, goodwill to Men' each year at Christmas. They are recalling the words of the angels who announced the birth of Jesus Christ in Bethlehem. For centuries, the town of Bethlehem had a mainly Christian population. In the early 21st century, however, Christians make up only about 12 per cent of the local population. Many have been driven away by years of fighting, and by the growing fundamentalism of their Muslim neighbours.

George Rabie, a young taxi driver from the outskirts of Bethlehem, believes that his Christianity puts him in daily danger. In 2006, he was beaten up by two young Muslim men who saw the crucifix (a depiction of Christ on the cross) on his windscreen. He explained how many people feel in an article called 'O, Muslim town of Bethlehem…' in *The Daily Mail* in 2006: 'Every day, I experience discrimination. It is a type of racism. We are a minority so we are an easier target. Many extremists from the villages are coming into Bethlehem.'

Other places can become flashpoints between fundamentalists of different faiths. Tension and even violence can flare up between Jewish and Muslim fundamentalists on the Temple Mount, a district of Jerusalem that is sacred to both faiths. Hindu and Sikh fundamentalists caused scores of deaths in the Indian state of Punjab in the 1970s and 1980s. The battle between Catholic and Protestant fundamentalists in Northern Ireland is another example.

1857–1859 Revolt against British rule in India is driven by Hindu and Muslim reaction to British practices >>>

1884–1885 Muhammad Ahmed (the Mahdi) drives Egyptians and British from Sudan in a move to promote purer Islam >>>

Chapter 2

The History of Fundamentalism

Seeds of conflict

When US President George W. Bush outlined his plans for a 'War on Terror' immediately after the 9/11 attacks in 2001, he used a religious term: 'this crusade, this war on terrorism, is going to take awhile'. Like many Americans, he might not have realised that he was using language that – to other believers – seemed tied to Christian fundamentalism.

For most Muslims, the word 'crusade' is deeply offensive and stirs up memories of vicious cruelty and fighting between the armies of Christianity and Islam. And the reason why a seemingly simple term can provoke so much suspicion lies at the heart of many religious conflicts around the world.

History is full of examples of religious clashes, with fundamentalists often stoking the flames of conflict. Jewish extremists led a full-scale revolt against their Roman rulers, leading to the destruction of Jerusalem in 70 CE. The Sikh religion developed in the 16th century in south Asia, partly to bring peace between Hindus and Muslims. Over the next 500 years, however, fundamentalists from each of those three faiths incited violence against one or both of the others.

Behind today's headlines

This book devotes much of its efforts to explaining the causes of tensions between Islamic fundamentalism and the non-Muslim world. Headlines around the world, after all, concentrate on these tensions, and the violence arising from them.

Islam, the faith professed by Muslims, arose in the 7th century. Around the year 610, according to Islamic tradition, an Arab merchant named Muhammad received messages direct from God. Within a few years, Muhammad began preaching some fundamental messages, that 'God is one' and that people should surrender to him. The Arabic word for 'surrender' is Islam.

Muhammad's message spread quickly through the Middle East, across North Africa and into southern Europe. The new believers memorised and wrote down the messages that Muhammad passed on; the written collection is known as the Koran. Muhammad and his followers did not believe that they had started a new religion. Instead, they believed they were calling people back to the true religion of the Bible's Old Testament. They believed that Muhammad was the last in a series of God's prophets, a series that included Abraham and Jesus.

Violent reaction

Warriors and preachers were the driving force in the spread of Islam. They established caliphates to rule Sicily, Spain and Portugal. The advance of Islam into Europe stopped in 732, when Christian

1481 Founding of the Spanish Inquisition >>> | **1618–1648** Catholic–Protestant conflict plays a major role in Europe's Thirty Years War >>> | **1869** Catholic Church declares that the Pope is infallible in matters of faith and morals >>>

8

This engraving, depicting Muhammad Ahmed (the Mahdi) at the time of the Muslim uprising in Sudan in the late 19th century, first appeared in the Illustrated London News.

guided by greed or violence, rather than by religious faith, and local populations suffered from their attacks. The Muslims regained most of the Holy Lands by about 1300, but by then many of them had come to consider Christians as cruel and barbarous.

Reawakening

From about 1500 to 1900, Muslim and Christian empires grew. The (Muslim) Ottoman Empire controlled much of the Middle East, south-eastern Europe and some of North Africa by the 19th century. By then, it had come into conflict with the rising European powers, especially Britain and France, which were eager to build their own empires.

armies defeated Muslim warriors at the Battle of Tours in western France. Most of Europe remained Christian, but most of the area that Christians considered as 'the Holy Lands' were in Muslim hands. Muslims also considered the area where Biblical events took place as sacred.

Eventually, European Christians decided to 'free' the Holy Lands from Muslim control by launching a series of invasions (called 'Crusades'), beginning in 1095. Many of these Europeans, however, were

The conflicts by the late 19th century had a new element: fundamentalism. In 1885, a group of dedicated Islamic fighters (whom we would now term 'fundamentalists') drove a British-Egyptian force out of Sudan. At around the same time, Christians in North America and Europe were edging towards the fundamentals of their own faith.

1910–1915 *The Fundamentals*, a 12-volume series of articles, promotes conservative Protestant beliefs >>>

The Shock of the New

Many people believe that the 20th century was the beginning of the Modern Era. Breakthroughs in science and technology saw people using telephones, cars and aeroplanes. Evidence seemed to support new theories that the Earth was billions of years old – and not simply thousands, as many Christians had believed. The theory of evolution proposed that human beings, like other living things, change over time and that we have evolved from our nearest animal relatives, the apes. Music, literature and painting all became more 'modern', abandoning centuries-old styles in favour of experimentation.

Profound response

With the pace of change so fast, religious believers – regardless of their faith – often felt unsettled and longed for reassurance. For many, this reassurance came with a return to their core beliefs. Christians were the first to put a name to this quest – fundamentalism. Curtis Lee Laws, an American minister, first used the word 'fundamentalists' in 1920 to describe people who shared his conservative religious views.

At about the same time, Muslims were looking to their past to find a way of living in the present. Islamic fundamentalism,

Schoolteacher John Thomas Scopes (second from left) went to trial in 1925 in the American state of Tennessee for teaching evolution. Christian fundamentalists wanted children to learn biblical accounts instead.

 1611 King James Bible (preferred version of English-speaking Christian fundamentalists) is published in England >>>

1870 Charles Hodge, an American opponent of evolution, publishes *What Is Darwinism?* >>>

like its Christian counterpart, is a reaction (to modernism, secularism, spiritual decline) as much as a force in itself. Fundamentalist groups formed across the Middle East, especially in Arabia and in Egypt. The Muslim Brotherhood, founded in Egypt in 1928 and promoting a fundamentalist agenda, spread from its religious roots to areas of politics, religion and education. With branches in more than 70 countries, it is now one of the most powerful Islamic organisations in the world.

QUOTE >

'God is our objective, the Koran is our Constitution, the Prophet is our leader, struggle is our way, and death for the sake of God is the highest of our aspirations.'

Motto of the Muslim Brotherhood (1928), as cited on the organisation's website www.ikhwanweb.com.

Repression and revolution

Many Islamic fundamentalists believe that the Koran should guide everything in life, including laws and forms of government. National boundaries would not mean much in their ideal world, which is why Islamic fundamentalist ideas pass easily throughout the Muslim world.

After World War II (WWII), the leaders of some mainly Muslim countries strengthened their ties with Western countries and their businesses. Fundamentalists disapproved of these ties, but their protests were often put down brutally. The ruler of Iran, for example, the Shah, was supported by the British and US governments. In turn, the Shah crushed any protests calling for stricter Muslim rule in his country.

Protests by Iranian fundamentalists became more widespread by the 1970s, and in early 1979 the Shah had to flee Iran. In February 1979, the Ayatollah Ruhollah Khomeini, a fundamentalist cleric, returned from exile and on 1 April 1979 Iranians voted to turn their country into an Islamic Republic. This series of events would have profound consequences within Iran and beyond in the decades to come.

Into the new century

The decades since Iran's Islamic Revolution have seen fundamentalism thrive all over the world. Other forms of Muslim fundamentalism, notably that of al Qaeda and the Taliban, have grabbed media attention.

Over the same period, though, Jewish fundamentalists have influenced Israeli government policy while the BJP (a fundamentalist Hindu political party) was India's dominant political party from 1998 to 2004. Fundamentalist Christians have grown in political power in the USA, helping form laws at state level and influencing the policies of the Republican party on a national level.

| **1879** Charles Taze Russell forms the Jehovah's Witnesses as a return to Christianity >>> | **1919** World's Christian Fundamentals Association is formed >>> | **1925** Scopes 'Monkey Trial' in USA denies the teaching of evolution in Tennessee schools >>> |

Case Study: Americans taken hostage at their embassy in Tehran

Mohammed Reza Pahlavi became Shah of Iran with the help of the United States of America and the Soviet Union (USSR) in 1941. He ruled for nearly four decades, modernising Iran and building ties with the West. He also crushed Islamic protests within Iran.

Islamic government

Eventually the protests grew too much, and the Shah and his family fled Iran in January 1979. The Islamic cleric Ayatollah Ruhollah Khomeini returned from exile to form an Islamic government. He urged Iranians to demonstrate against 'the great Satan' and 'the Enemy of Islam', as he described the USA.

Decisive action

On 4 November 1979, radical Islamic students stormed the US Embassy in Tehran and took 66 people hostage. The USA was outraged, believing that the action broke internationally agreed customs that protect embassy officials.

The Iranians released a few hostages in the first few weeks, but held on to the others for several months. A rescue attempt in April 1980 failed when a US helicopter crashed into a transport plane in the Iranian desert.

Many Americans became angry with President Jimmy Carter's 'weakness'. He was defeated by Ronald Reagan in the presidential election of November 1980.

One of Carter's last acts as president was to agree to a release plan that called for billions of dollars 'frozen' by US banks and a US promise not to interfere in Iran. The 52 remaining hostages were released on 20 January 1981.

The fundamentalist captors presented some of the American hostages to the public after releasing them following several weeks of captivity. Others would remain captive for 14 more months.

WHAT THE WORLD THINKS...

These are three articles from publications around the
world commenting on the hostage situation in 1979.
Compare and contrast the various viewpoints and see
if you can find any more newspaper reports or other
media discussing Iran.

Arbeiter Zeitung, 6 November 1979

'It is impossible to
foresee how the affair
in Tehran will end. The
problem is that, for the
USA, giving in to the
demands of the
hostage-takers is just
as difficult to accept as
the threatened fate of
its countrymen.'

Arbeiter Zeitung is an Austrian daily
newspaper.

Ayatollah Ruhollah Khomeini, quoted in *Khomeini: Life of the Ayatollah*, 7 November 1979

'This action has many benefits.
We keep the hostages, finish our
internal work, then release them.
We can put the constitution to the
people's vote without difficulty,
and carry out presidential and
parliamentary elections. When we
have finished all these jobs, we can
let the hostages go.'

Ayatollah Khomeini was speaking to Iranian Foreign
Minister Abolhassan Bani Sadr.

Time magazine, 17 December 1979

'For five long weeks they have been held under threat
of death in the U.S. embassy in Tehran. Their arms have
been bound, and they have been forbidden to speak to
one another. Their captors have subjected them to
intense questioning, and even threatened some of them
at gunpoint. All the while, crowds of fanatical followers
of the Ayatullah Ruhollah Khomeini have demonstrated
outside the embassy walls.'

Chapter 3

The Causes of Fundamentalism

Understanding fundamentalism

Peaceful coexistence, devoted study and a quest to behave well are not the sort of subjects that grab headlines or lead on the television evening news. And yet these are the very qualities that draw many believers to become fundamentalists – no matter what their religious beliefs are. The media is more interested in conflicts between rival fundamentalist groups or between fundamentalists and non-religious governments.

A Jew might be drawn to fundamentalism by the words of a rabbi or by studying religious writings. Hindus can find a path to inner peace by becoming absorbed in religious ceremonies. Christians might be inspired to explore fundamentalism through the persuasive words of a preacher appearing on television or conducting a service in a church holding thousands of worshippers.

Even the media can understand that the routes to fundamentalism are varied, and that the goal of most fundamentalists is a peaceful one. The big media blind spot, however, is Islam.

Understanding Islam

Some Muslims – and probably most of that small minority that is involved with terrorism – believe that there is no such thing as Islamic fundamentalism. For them, to believe in the Muslim message automatically means being what others would call a fundamentalist. They are guided by the Islamic principle of sharia, which sets out guidelines for most aspects of life, including politics, banking, diet, family life and business.

Many people use the term Islamism to describe such an all-inclusive interpretation of the Koran and Islam itself. Islamists might well be fundamentalists in their private set of beliefs, but it is how they behave in public that makes the difference. Islamists take the core guidelines of Islam and aim to create societies that operate 100 per cent within these guidelines. Sometimes, as in the case of the Taliban in Afghanistan, this means making strict laws against women's rights and crushing traces of the non-Muslim past.

Other routes to fundamentalism

Christians and Muslims are not the only believers to be drawn to fundamentalism. Many Orthodox Jews believe that Jewish people have a special relationship with God; some Orthodox Jews use this belief to justify any action taken by Israel against non-Jews, especially Muslims.

Some Hindus in India are drawn to fundamentalism because they blame changes in their country and the world on Islamic terrorism and the influence of Western countries. For example, Hindu fundamentalists destroyed a mosque in Ayodhya (Gujarat state) in 1992.

610-622 The Prophet Muhammad receives visions and preaches in Arabia >>> | **632** Muhammad dies; Abu Bakr (Muhammad's closest friend) chosen as caliph >>> | **632** Sunni–Shia split develops over Muhammad's successor >>>

14

Even Buddhism, a religion associated with patience and tolerance, has a fundamentalist dimension. Hard-line Buddhists in Sri Lanka sometimes target Hindus and their temples in an attempt to rid their country of 'foreign influences'.

Despite their obvious differences in actual beliefs, these fundamentalist groups share a number of attitudes. One of the most important is a suspicion of change, which can also mean a hostile attitude towards foreign influence. Progress, whether it is economic or social, undermines these fundamentalist values. Fundamentalists therefore view the past as a more peaceful and happier time.

Each year, millions of Muslims make a pilgrimage (or Haj) to the holy city of Mecca. Devout Muslims view the Haj as a scared obligation, and believers have a duty to complete it at least once in their lifetime.

633 Wars of conquest begin >>> 650 Caliph Uthman orders that the Koran be written down >>> 680 Foundation of the Shia sect of Islam >>> 1193 Death of military Saladin sees nearly all of the Holy Land once more under Muslim control >>>

Turning Belief into Action

One of the most important features of religious fundamentalism is faith. That one word was one of the most important sources of conflict during the Reformation in Europe in the 16th century. Many Jews, Christians and Muslims view faith as it is defined in the Old Testament (which is considered sacred by all groups): 'Now faith is the substance of things hoped for, the evidence of things not seen'.

Fundamentalists of all religious groups use this understanding of faith to promote their own views and to defend themselves against criticisms from those who do not share a fundamentalist outlook. The core of their belief – that sacred writings or traditions provide the answers for everything in life – is enforced with this view. When sceptics argue with them, saying that there is no scientific proof or justification for fundamentalism, they respond by accusing the sceptics of lacking faith. The opponents in such an argument find little common ground to shift the other's opinion.

QUOTE >

'The overarching theme to the fundamentalist, whether Muslim or Christian, is that God is to be worshipped, respected, feared & obeyed above all else… This intense and abiding devotion means that there are some things that are completely, utterly non-negotiable. In this way, it is like viewing the world as being black and white, with little if any gray between that which is good and that which is evil.'

American psychologist **M. E. Nielsen**, *North American Journal of Psychology*, 2002.

Spreading the word

Religious fundamentalism would not be a global issue if fundamentalists kept to themselves and cherished their beliefs quietly. But just looking at national newspapers or television news broadcasts for a week should convince anyone that fundamentalism really is an issue in the news – both nationally and internationally.

Many fundamentalists believe that it is wrong not to spread the 'good news' that they have to offer. They feel a duty to spread this news, convincing others of its merits and making the world more receptive to it. For them, spreading the word about their beliefs is more than simply convincing the world about their faith – it is offering people their only chance of salvation.

Fundamentalists, who believe that their set of values should apply around the world, face this pressure every day. They feel that they should influence the wider world, but need to find a way of

| 1453 Mehmet Fatih conquers Constantinople and establishes (Muslim) Ottoman Empire >>> | 1703 Birth of Muhammad ibn Abd al-Wahhab at-Tamimi, Islamic reformer >>> | 1927–1929 The Wahhabi Ikhwan, Muslim fundamentalists, revolt against Arabian ruler ibn Saud >>> |

16

doing it forcefully. Media reports on terrorist attacks often overlook the fact that the terrorists, at least in their own eyes, believe that they are doing the work of God.

Sometimes, fundamentalists employ some of the same tools and techniques that they would otherwise oppose as being anti-religious or not in keeping with their beliefs. In this way, new means of communication can either be hated or absorbed. Islamic fundamentalists, for example, have begun

Young fundamentalists burn an effigy during a violent demonstration in Indonesia. As the country with the largest Muslim population in the world, Indonesia also has one of the largest (and youngest) populations of Islamic fundamentalists.

broadcasting on television stations in the same way that their Christian counterparts have done for some time. And the Internet – sometimes condemned as providing those deemed to be sinners with a mouthpiece – can also be put to use spreading the fundamentalist message.

| **1928** Muslim Brotherhood is founded in Egypt >>> | **1979** Iranian revolutionaries overthrow the Shah and establish a Muslim government >>> | **1990s** Taliban (fundamentalists) comes to power in Afghanistan >>> |

Case Study: Osama bin Laden, founder of al Qaeda

Osama bin Laden was born in 1957 in Saudi Arabia. His father was a wealthy building contractor. While at King Abdulaziz University, bin Laden became influenced by activists who called for a united Muslim front against non-Muslim enemies.

Choosing his enemies

In the early 1980s, bin Laden joined armed Muslim rebels as they drove Soviet soldiers from Afghanistan. He recruited thousands of other Muslims to the cause and became leader of al Qaeda, which was formed in 1988.

When the Soviets were driven from Afghanistan in 1989, bin Laden returned to Saudi Arabia. He was expelled in 1991 after criticising the Saudi government for allowing non-Muslim elements – especially US and other Western soldiers – into Saudi Arabia. Bin Laden spent five years in Sudan before returning to Afghanistan, where he continued to train al Qaeda volunteers.

Al Qaeda was linked to a number of attacks on US interests, including an attempt to blow up the New York World Trade Center in 1993, the 1996 attack on US forces in Saudi Arabia (killing 20) and attacks on US embassies in Kenya and Tanzania in 2000, claiming 200 victims.

Most importantly, bin Laden and al Qaeda have been the chief suspects for the 11 September 2001 ('9/11') terrorist attacks on the United States of America. Since 2001, Osama bin Laden has remained in hiding, probably in Afghanistan or Pakistan. Meanwhile, al Qaeda still claims responsibility for attacks on the West, including deadly attacks on Madrid (2004) and London (2005).

Osama bin Laden, pictured here in a cave hideout, has eluded capture for more than seven years since the 9/11 attacks on America.

WHAT THE WORLD THINKS...

These are three articles from publications around the world commenting on Osama bin Laden. Compare and contrast the various viewpoints and see if you can find any more newspaper reports or other media discussing the al Qaeda fundamentalist.

Islamic Republic News Agency, 16 September 2001

'Killing of people, in any place and with any kind of weapons…carried out by any organization, country or individual is condemned…It makes no difference whether such massacres happen in Hiroshima, Nagasaki, Qana, Sabra, Shatila, Deir Yassin, Bosnia, Kosovo, Iraq or in New York and Washington.'

The Islamic Republic News Agency represents the views of the Iranian government.

Abubakar Mujahid, BBC News website, Ja'amutu Tajidmul Islami, The Movement for Islamic Revival (Nigeria) 1 October 2001

'America has yet to publish any evidence and if instead it is determined to go the cowboy way with two guns blazing to get Osama bin Laden dead or alive, it will definitely lead to a confrontation between America and the Islamic world.'

Abubakar Mujahid is the leader of Ja'amutu Tajidmul Islami, The Movement for Islamic Revival in Nigeria.

Newsweek, 15 October 2001

'For [Osama bin Laden] and his followers, this is a holy war between Islam and the Western world. Most Muslims disagree. Every Islamic country in the world has condemned the attacks of September 11. To many, bin Laden belongs to a long line of extremists who have invoked religion to justify mass murder and spur men to suicide.'

Chapter 4

The Impact of Fundamentalism

Life in a fundamentalist society

What would it be like to live in a world shaped by fundamentalism? The answer is easier to find than it seems at first, because fundamentalists have come to control many societies throughout history (even if they might not have called themselves fundamentalists). Moreover, several of today's countries are governed along fundamentalist lines.

Shared values

One of the legacies of the Roman Empire was the Christian religion. Even as they descended into the 'Dark Ages' at the beginning of the Medieval period, European countries shared their basic Christian beliefs. At times, groups of Medieval protesters would accuse their societies of having lost track of basic Christian values. Some of these groups, labelled heretics by the Church, would draw away from society and form their own communities.

Others would set about changing the communities where they lived. In the late 15th century, for example, the hard-line priest Girolamo Savonarola gained followers – and, briefly, political control – in the rich Italian city-state of Florence. Savonarola persuaded Florentines to burn their luxury goods in a 'bonfire of vanities'.

Christians continued to press for purer, 'basic' societies after the Reformation as well. John Calvin turned the Swiss city of Geneva into a stronghold of conservative Protestant values. The Pilgrims in the USA, escaping religious persecution in England, set up an equally strict and intolerant society in Massachusetts. Quakers – members of a peaceful, but rival Protestant sect – were whipped, sentenced to hard labour or driven from Massachusetts.

> **QUOTE >**
>
> 'No [red] hat shall I have but that of a martyr, reddened with my own blood.'
>
> **Girolamo Savonarola** refusing the office of cardinal (one level below the Pope in the Catholic clergy), 'Puritan in Florence', *Time* magazine, 2 June 1952.

Other Protestant groups continue to uphold fundamentalist traditions that were formed centuries ago. The Mennonite people in the American states of Pennsylvania and Ohio live in close-knit communities that look to the Bible for inspiration and guidance. The most extreme members of this group, the Amish, refuse to use any technology developed after the 17th century. They don't use electricity and automobiles and wear simple clothing, even using clasps instead of zips.

Modern Islam

Nowadays, fundamentalists continue to influence some elements in Western countries, especially the USA. But it is Islam that leads the way in producing outright fundamentalist societies. Iran, Saudi Arabia and Sudan are governed with strict Islamic law at their heart.

These fundamentalist societies depend on interpretations of the Koran to decide how laws will be made and enforced. In Saudi Arabia, for example, women are denied many things that women in other countries consider to be 'rights', such as driving, travelling freely and dressing as they choose. Iranians can still be stoned to death as a legal punishment for certain sex crimes.

Islamic law extends to other areas in such countries, areas where religion plays no part in much of the world. Sharia law, which extends to most areas of human behaviour, sets strict limits on how Muslims should act at all times. These limits and the harsh punishments that can follow seem cruel and even outdated to some outsiders. But, as the BBC notes, many Muslims 'see the Sharia not in the light of something primitive but as something divinely revealed'.

Two women, masked and covered from head to toe, sit in the boot of a car during the Taliban rule of Afghanistan, which ran from 1996 to 2001. The Taliban had an extreme interpretation of Muslim tradition, imposing strict limitations on women.

Muslims in the West

The Western media sometimes implies that every Islamic fundamentalist is out to undermine the basic freedoms and human rights that people struggled for centuries to achieve. This view is not accurate and very often it is the conservative Muslims who seem to have a hard time living their lives freely in the West. American Muslims have had to endure insults and violence since the 9/11 terror attacks, but Muslims in other Western countries also face enormous challenges.

Many young African-Americans have joined the Nation of Islam, a religious group with strict rules on dress and behaviour.

'Rights' and wrongs

Many of the things that Muslims value, such as abstaining from alcohol and conservative clothes for women, set them apart from their neighbours. And rather than simply viewing these Muslim customs

as different, some Westerners consider them threatening. Several European countries, especially France and Britain, have had long-running disputes centring on what clothing Muslim children can wear to school (see pages 24–25). Women's clothing, including veils to cover the face, is also a source of heated discussion.

Jack Straw, a senior minister in the British government, entered this debate very publicly in October 2006. Writing in a local newspaper in Blackburn (his constituency), he described how uncomfortable he had felt having an interview with a local Muslim woman whose face was covered by a veil. As reported in the *Lancashire Evening Telegraph*, he felt that Muslim women lost the chance to be part of their local communities because of the veil: 'Above all, it was because I felt uncomfortable about talking to someone "face-to-face" who I could not see. So I decided that I wouldn't just sit there the next time a

> **QUOTE >**
>
> 'I come to this out of a profound commitment to equal rights for Muslim communities and an equal concern about adverse development about parallel communities.'
>
> **Jack Straw**, Leader of the House, 'Today' programme, BBC Radio 4, 6 October 2006.

| 1930 Nation of Islam founded in the USA >>> | 1926 The Koran declared to be the Saudi Arabian constitution >>> | 1947 Pakistan founded as an Islamic nation >>> | 1979 Iran becomes an Islamic republic >>> |

22

Muslim schoolgirls in the UK wear scarves and other clothing to reflect their religious background.

lady turned up to see me in a full veil, and I haven't.'

French newspapers, radio stations and television programmes have also debated whether Muslims who seem to separate themselves so much through their customs, behaviour and appearance can really be considered fully French. Like many in Britain, they feel that Muslims are abusing their human rights by choosing not to blend into society.

Sticks and stones

Some Muslims find that the long arm of fundamentalism can follow them into more tolerant societies. Salman Rushdie was born into an Indian Muslim family, but living in Britain when he wrote a book called *The Satanic Verses* in 1988. The book offended many Muslims, including Iran's senior cleric Ayatollah Khomeini, who believed that the book was blasphemous.

Khomeini took his disapproval much further, though, and issued a fatwa (an Islamic legal ruling) calling on Muslims to kill Rushdie and his publishers. Rushdie was forced into hiding for years, living in secret locations. The fatwa was no empty threat: in 1991, the book's Japanese translator, Hitoshi Igarashi, was stabbed to death. The Italian and Norwegian translators survived similar knife attacks. Rushdie has lived his life more openly in recent years but the fatwa still stands, even though Khomeini died four months after issuing it.

1989 Iran's Ayatollah Khomeini issues fatwa calling for Salman Rushdie's death >>>

1996 Taliban movement establishes Islamic rule in Afghanistan >>>

2005 The deaths of two Muslim teenagers trigger two months of rioting in suburbs of Paris >>>

Case Study: Shabina Begum, Muslim schoolgirl in England

On 3 September 2002, 14-year-old Shabina Begum arrived at Denbigh High School in Luton dressed in a jilbab, a long gown that hides the body's shape beneath it. She was accompanied by her older 19-year-old brother and his friend. Together, they tried to persuade the assistant head teacher to allow Shabina to wear the jilbab, even though it was not allowed as part of the school's uniform policy.

Shabina was told to go home and change into the school uniform, which she had worn for the previous two years at the same school. Shabina and her brother hired a solicitor to encourage the school and the local education authority to relax the school uniform. They said that Shabina's religious beliefs – and by extension, her human rights – were denied by having to wear the uniform.

For more than two years, Shabina stayed out of school while her case gained publicity. A British High Court decision in June 2004 supported the school's policy. Eventually, Shabina returned to a local school that allowed the jilbab. But her case continued, with Cherie Booth, a successful barrister and wife of then-Prime Minister Tony Blair, agreeing to take it on. The British Court of Appeal reversed the earlier decision (deciding in favour of the schoolgirl) in March 2005.

The case then went to the Law Lords – in effect, the highest court in Britain. In March 2006, the Law Lords unanimously decided that Denbigh High School had acted legally in its enforcement of the dress code.

Shabina Begum became a symbol of the conflict between religious and secular influences in British society. Her case stirred public opinion far beyond Luton – or even Britain.

2004 French government passes law banning the wearing of religious symbols in state schools >>>

2006 High-level debate in the UK about Islamic women's veils >>>

March 2006 British Muslim schoolgirl Shabina Begum loses the right to wear the *jilbab* at school >>>

WHAT THE WORLD THINKS...

These are three articles from publications around the world concerning the conflict surrounding Shabina Begum and the clothes she wore to school. Compare and contrast the various viewpoints and see if you can find any more newspaper reports or other media discussing the case.

The Telegraph,
23 March 2006

'This case wasn't even about religion, or conscience, or the dictates of faith. At least It wasn't primarily about those things. It was about power. It was about who really runs the schools in this country, and about how far militant Islam could go in bullying the poor, cowed...apparatus of the British state.'

The National Review,
28 March 2005

'In the long annals of judicial stupidity, there can rarely have been a more idiotic judgment than that recently given by Lord Justice Brooke of the British Court of Appeal [supporting Shabina Begum]. It reads like the suicide note not of a country alone, but of an entire civilization.'

The National Review is an American magazine.

Word Press website,
24 March 2006

'Shabina Begum's right to wear the jilbab infringed upon no other person's rights, denying her that right infringes upon the rights of 3% of the British population.'

Word Press website www.wordpress.com is a blog-hosting website.

Crossing boundaries

It was only in the last decades of the 20th century that fundamentalism, especially Islamic fundamentalism, came to capture the world's attention and to dominate headlines. And the words that so often accompany the phrase 'Islamic fundamentalism' in these reports are 'terror' and 'terrorism'.

Battle lines

Just how and why did Islamic fundamentalism become so linked (in many people's view) with terror and bloodshed? The answer is complicated, but some of the reasons can be traced to the nature of any fundamentalism. Most people agree that fundamentalism is strongest, and gains new recruits, when people feel that their beliefs are threatened.

By the 1970s, many Muslims felt that growing Western influence in their countries had weakened their national identities, and that people were in danger of drifting away from their faith. Another, more political issue also captured their attention: the plight of the Palestinian people. Thousands of Palestinians (mainly Muslims) had been moved from their lands when the state of Israel was founded in 1948. For decades, many of those Palestinians continued to live in refugee camps. The Arab- Israeli wars of 1948, 1956, 1967 and 1973 had done little to improve conditions for Palestinians – or to find a peaceful solution to the 'Middle East problem'.

Many Islamic fundamentalists had come to blame the USA for both of these areas of conflict by the late 1970s. As the most powerful and richest Western country, the

Rescue workers survey the damage caused by the terrorist explosion on the Indonesian island of Bali in 2005. The targets were Western visitors and the businesses that catered to them.

| **1993** Car bomb at World Trade Center kills six and injures 1,042 >>> | **1996** Attack on Americans in Saudi Arabia kills 20 and injures 372 >>> | **1998** Bombs at US embassies in Kenya and Tanzania kill 220-plus >>> | **2001** 3,000-plus die in '9/11' in the USA >>> |

A London policeman stands outside an Underground station following the terrorist attack on 7 July 2005. Muslim fundamentalists attacked three Underground trains and a bus, killing 56 and injuring 700 people.

USA was able to spread its influence across the globe, even to traditionally Muslim regions. Also, the USA was – and remains – Israel's closest ally, supplying it with billions of dollars' worth of aid and weapons.

The new generation of Islamic fundamentalists was angry, and it had found an opponent. Plus, many young Muslims in Western countries began travelling to fundamentalist strongholds in Afghanistan and Sudan. There they received training and strengthened their aim to spread the fundamentalist message further.

Terror campaigns

The Islamic Revolution in Iran in 1979 and the Taliban victory over Soviet armed forces in Afghanistan a decade later inspired other Islamic fundamentalists to carry the battle to the West. Israel, the USA and their allies were the main targets, but the terrorist tactics saw people from many other countries die.

The two US-led invasions of Iraq, in 1991 and 2003, turned many fundamentalists even further against the USA. Bit by bit, the stage was set for the series of anti-Western (and especially anti-American) terrorist attacks of the 1990s and into the new century.

> **QUOTE >**
>
> 'Larger numbers of terrorist recruits left Britain during the late 1990s to fight the "holy war" in Bosnia, Chechnya and Afghanistan. The number of Britons estimated to have travelled to terror training camps in Afghanistan before 2002 has been put as high as 3,000 by MI5 [the UK national security agency].'
>
> **Eliza Manningham-Buller** cited, director-general of MI5, '70 British Muslims join Iraq fighters', *The Sunday Times*, 26 June 2005.

> **2002** Bali bombing kills 200-plus >>> | **2004** Madrid train bombings kill 192 and wound 2050 >>> | **July 2005** Attacks on London's public transport kill 56 and wound 700 >>> | **Oct 2005** Second Bali bombing kills 23 >>>

27

Chapter 5

Responses to Fundamentalism

The War on Terror

The terrorist attacks on 11 September 2001 killed nearly 3,000 people in the USA, but had far-reaching consequences around the world. From the start, the US government blamed the Islamic fundamentalist terror group al Qaeda (and its leader Osama bin Laden) for the attack (see pages 18–19).

Within three days of 9/11, the US Congress approved President Bush's plan to 'use all necessary and appropriate force' to find and punish those who were responsible for the attacks. The last time the USA had been attacked so suddenly was on 7 December 1941 during World War II. Then, it had responded by immediately declaring war on Japan.

The 9/11 attacks were different. Al Qaeda is a secretive organisation and not a country. But President Bush did have a country in mind: Afghanistan, whose fundamentalist Muslim government (known as the Taliban) offered support and hiding places to al Qaeda. And Bush had a name in mind as well: the War on Terror.

Into Afghanistan

On 7 October 2001, US combat troops entered Afghanistan. Their mission was to drive the Taliban government from power and to cripple any al Qaeda activity within Afghanistan. The troops had no doubts that they were also

QUOTE >

'Women are not allowed to attend school. You can be jailed for owning a television. Religion can be practised only as their leaders dictate. A man can be jailed in Afghanistan if his beard is not long enough.'

US President **George W. Bush** addressing the US Congress, 20 September 2001.

NATO troops patrol a neighbourhood suspected of hiding Taliban supporters and other fundamentalist opponents in Afghanistan, 2002.

14 Sept 2001 US Congress allows President Bush to use 'all necessary and appropriate force' against those who committed or helped the 9/11 attacks >>>

7 Oct 2001 US troops go to Afghanistan >>>

The USA has detained 558 people suspected of planning terrorist activities in a special centre in Guantanamo, part of the island of Cuba under US control. Most detainees are Muslim.

hunting for al Qaeda leader Osama bin Laden – 'dead or alive'.

In over seven years of involvement within Afghanistan, the War on Terror has had some successes as well as some setbacks. The Taliban have been swept from power and Afghanistan saw its first free elections for three decades in 2004 and 2005. Many experts believe that al Qaeda has been weakened, even if Osama bin Laden remains at large. However, US and other troops in the North American Treaty Organisation (NATO) still remain in Afghanistan because of an increasing fundamentalist backlash against foreign troops. In addition, many Muslims across the world protest against the US policy of taking suspected terrorists captured in Afghanistan and sending them to a detention centre in Cuba to be questioned by US forces.

Operation Enduring Freedom

The five main US-led operations in the War on Terror are known collectively as Operation Enduring Freedom. They are:

Operation Enduring Freedom – Afghanistan (OEF-A): dealing with al Qaeda, Taliban and other fundamentalist groups.

Operation Enduring Freedom – Philippines (OEF-P): about 350 US troops helping fight al Qaeda and allied Muslim rebel groups.

Operation Enduring Freedom – Horn of Africa (OEF-HOA): combating al Qaeda and other groups in and around Somalia with NATO allies.

Operation Enduring Freedom – Trans Sahara (OEF-TS): combating al Qaeda elements in the region with North African allies.

Operation Enduring Freedom – Pankisi Gorge: from 2002 to 2004, the US helped train soldiers in the Asian country of Georgia in anti-terrorism techniques.

 26 Oct 2001 US Patriot Act allows more government investigation of individuals >>> | **2002** First foreign terrorist suspects arrive at Guantanamo >>> | **2004** Reports of Coalition cruelty at Abu Ghraib jail, Baghdad >>>

Iraq

Less than two years after sending troops into Afghanistan in the wake of 9/11, the USA led an invasion of another Muslim country, Iraq. President George W. Bush did not directly blame Iraq for the 9/11 actions; he did, however, suggest that Iraqi leader Saddam Hussein gave al Qaeda terrorists shelter and possibly direct support. Moreover, he believed that Saddam Hussein's government possessed weapons of mass destruction, which Iraq could use against the outside world.

The USA, backed by 48 other countries (four of which sent attacking troops), formed the 'Coalition of the Willing' in 2003. The aim of the coalition was to invade Iraq and overthrow Saddam Hussein, replacing him with elected officials. Saddam Hussein had been almost an ally of the West in the 1980s, when he led a war against fundamentalist Iran. But from the early 1990s (when an earlier US-led invasion drove Iraqi invaders from Kuwait), he had become its enemy.

Tougher than expected

On 20 March 2003, Coalition forces attacked Iraq and soon gained control of the capital, Baghdad. President Bush said 'Mission accomplished' to US forces in the region. In mid-December 2003, Saddam Hussein was captured and faced a lengthy trial. He was convicted of war crimes and executed on 30 December 2006.

However, events in Iraq began to take unexpected turns. Even if the invasion had not been aimed at Iraq because it is a Muslim country, many Muslims came to view it in those terms. Muslims who had no love for Saddam Hussein began to criticise the invasion as an attack on Islam. Many moderates – inside Iraq and beyond its borders – were drawn to militant fundamentalism. Parts of Iraq, including large areas within Baghdad itself – proved hard to govern.

From 2004 onwards, the media reported suicide bombings, attacks on occupying troops and general unrest – almost on a daily basis. Hard-line fundamentalists found it easy to recruit supporters to take

President George W. Bush travelled to the Middle East to pronounce 'Mission accomplished' after invading Iraq in 2003.

20 March 2003 US and British troops enter Iraq >>> | **August 2003** Deadly bomb attack on UN headquarters in Baghdad >>> | **14 December 2003** Saddam Hussein is captured in Tikrit >>>

30

Iraqi police (behind shields) demonstrate their skills in a riot-control display in January 2008. Rival fundamentalist groups have grown powerful in Iraq since the US-led invasion of 2003.

on the Coalition forces. Fundamentalist cleric Moqtada Sadr, who has called for a national uprising against foreign troops, has strongholds in the city of Falluja and in parts of Baghdad.

By mid-2008, the United States still had about 140,000 troops in Iraq. And although 2007 had seen some progress in restoring peace to Iraq's 'hot spots', it also was the worst year for US causalities. By 31 December, 899 Americans had died in action in Iraq during 2007, 49 more than had died in the second-worst year, 2004. Iraq looked set to remain an explosive issue.

> ### QUOTE >
>
> 'The reason we armed Saddam Hussein is because he was seen as an absolutely fundamental interest of the west against rising Muslim fundamentalism based in Iran. We have destabilised Iraq, greatly empowered Iran and the dangers to us in that process have been very considerably increased.'
>
> **Michael Heseltine**, former UK Defence Secretary, 'Question Time' on the BBC, 8 November 2007.

2004–2006 Sunni and Shia followers bomb each other, as well as attacking Coaliton forces, killing hundreds in Iraq >>>

30 Dec 2006 Saddam Hussein executed >>>

August 2007 Kurdish and Shia leaders form an alliance, but Sunnis refuse to join >>>

Muslim fault lines

The West is not alone in coming to terms with Islamic fundamentalism and its

Thousands of Turks carry flags and posters of Mustafa Kemal Ataturk (founder of modern Turkey) during an election rally in 2007. Ataturk promoted a non-religious government, but some modern Turks want a stronger role for Islam.

political consequences. Many of the worst acts of violence take place within Muslim communities or Muslim states.

Hatred of compromise

Iraq, with its horrifying series of car bombs and kidnappings, is one obvious flash point. Television viewers around the world

1889 Ahmadiyya Muslim Community, a reform movement, founded in India >>>	1914 Lahore Ahmadiyya Movement splits from the Ahmadiyya Muslim Community >>>	1924 Kemal Ataturk closes Islamic courts and abolishes Islamic law in Turkey >>>

see the results of fundamentalist-inspired violence. Some of this violence flares up in response to US and other foreign forces being posted in Iraq. Other terrorist acts reflect the bitter divisions within Iraq's own Muslim communities.

Other Islamic countries, however, also face enormous tensions from within. Pakistan, Turkey, Egypt, Saudi Arabia and Indonesia are all Muslim-majority states with constitutions and laws that reflect their Islamic heritage. Nevertheless, each has felt a profound fundamentalist backlash because of 'compromises' (in the eyes of the fundamentalists).

These compromises can take many forms. Saudi fundamentalists, notably Osama bin Laden, are furious that the Saudi government has allowed foreigners (and especially non-Muslim troops) into the most sacred land of Islam. Many Turks resent the secular constitution that has been in place for a century. Egyptian fundamentalists disapprove of the harsh treatment that the Muslim Brotherhood receives there – the result, they say, of the government's eagerness to stay in 'America's good books'.

Dialogue and conflict

Other societies around the world are trying to find new ways to deal with fundamentalism. Scientific and secular (non-religious) groups in the USA are struggling against a growing trend by Christian fundamentalists to promote a biblical view of science. Israelis seeking peace with their Palestinian (and

mainly Muslim) neighbours try to reduce the influence of Jewish fundamentalists in the Israeli parliament. India faces continued tensions between its government (which is meant to be non-religious) and the country's powerful fundamentalist Hindu and Sikh communities.

Teddy's big adventure

An incident in late 2007 shed light on what the Western media calls the 'fanatic' attitudes of Islamic fundamentalists. Less obviously, though, it pointed out how having a shared faith can help with diplomacy.

A British woman, Gillian Gibbons, had been teaching in a school in Khartoum, the capital of Sudan (which has a fundamentalist Muslim government). In September 2007, she asked the six- and seven-year-old children to name a teddy bear she had brought in. The children decided on the name 'Muhammad'. On 25 November, Mrs Gibbons was arrested and charged with 'insulting religion' (because the great Islamic prophet is named Muhammad)

Four days later Mrs Gibbon was found guilty and sent to jail for a 15-day sentence. British and Western journalists were shocked at her treatment. Meanwhile, Sudanese fundamentalists began protesting that her sentence was too light. Some called for her to be executed, chanting loudly 'No tolerance, execution' and 'Kill her, kill her by firing squad'.

On 1 December, two British Muslim peers, Baroness Warsi and Lord Ahmed, arrived in Sudan to plead on behalf of Mrs Gibbons. Sudan's President, Omar al-Bashir, met them and two days later pardoned Mrs Gibbons, who was allowed to fly back to Britain.

| 1941 Islamist political party Jamaat-e-Islami founded in (modern) Pakistan >>> | 1953 Pakistan declares martial law in Lahore after Ahmadiyya riots >>> | 1982 Hezbollah founded in Lebanon >>> |

33

Case Study: Abu Hamza, the fundamentalist cleric

The hard-line cleric Abu Hamza, with his missing eye and hook, symbolises the hatred and aggression of Muslim fundamentalists – in the eyes of many in the West. Many observers believe that his fiery sermons have led young Muslim men down the path of violence.

The path to extremism

Abu Hamza was born Mustafa Kamel Mustafa in Alexandria, Egypt, in 1958. He entered the UK in 1979 to study engineering and became a British citizen in 1983. Abu Hamza was inspired by the Islamic Revolution in Iran, and its opposition to the USA.

Abu Hamza travelled to Afghanistan to join the anti-Soviet Mujahideen movement in 1989. He stayed on after the Russians left, losing his hands and one eye while clearing landmines. In 1995, Hamza went to support Bosnian Muslims during the break-up of Yugoslavia.

In 1997, Abu Hamza returned to Britain and began preaching at the Finsbury Park Mosque in London. British police and security forces watched him closely. Hamza was questioned about bombings in Yemen, but continued to preach a message of extremism – including support for 9/11.

In August 2004, Abu Hamza was arrested, and on 7 February 2006 was convicted of stirring up racial hatred and promoting murder. On 15 November 2007, a British judge ruled that he could be extradited to the USA , to face serious terrorist charges. If convicted there, he could be sentenced to 99 years in prison.

Fundamentalist cleric Abu Hamza drew the attention of the British media and devout Muslims in equal measure whenever he preached at the Finsbury Park mosque in London.

WHAT THE WORLD THINKS...

These are three articles from newspapers around the world commenting on the Abu Hamza and his teachings. Compare and contrast the various viewpoints and see if you can find any more newspaper reports or other media discussing him.

The Independent, 22 January 2003

'Despite the fact that I find this terrifying beyond measure, I have to say it isn't hard to see the appeal of Finsbury Park mosque to young Muslims. Abu Hamza is charismatic and particularly good at listening to young men who everywhere else are shunned. He offers the one thing that all angst-crippled teenagers crave: certainty, and a clear path through life.'

The Daily Telegraph, 28 May 2004

'I am ready to defend the right of Abu Hamza to a fair trial. Am I, though, prepared to defend his right to incite young Muslims to join al-Qa'eda's global jihad against the Judaeo-Christian West – if that is indeed what he has done? No: he has no such right, and nor does anybody else. Abu Hamza can be my neighbour or my enemy: he cannot expect to be both.'

Al-Ahram Weekly, 3-9 June 2004

'With his inflammatory rhetoric and his hook instead of a right-hand, Abu Hamza was an irresistible target for Britain's tabloid press, always on the look out for figures to plausibly confirm their own prejudices. For his part, Abu Hamza revelled in his notoriety.'

Al-Ahram is an Egyptian newspaper.

Chapter 6

Fundamentalism and the Media

The new Cold War

Following the end of WWII, the world lived in a state of constant tension. Two countries, the United States and the Soviet Union (USSR), represented opposing political systems and were far more powerful than any others. These 'superpowers' kept arming themselves, preparing for an all-out war with the other country.

That all-out war never came, because it would have destroyed both countries – and possibly the whole world. Instead, the world endured the 'Cold War', more than four decades of nervous expectation. Neither superpower ever invaded the o ther; instead their dispute was played out by their allies. The Soviet Union helped rebels trying to overthrow the government of a US ally, and the United States did the same for anti-Soviet fighters.

Each superpower became directly involved in – and ultimately lost – lengthy conflicts in other countries. US forces left Vietnam in 1975 after failing hold back pro-Soviet forces there for more than 10 years. And the Soviet army left Afghanistan, defeated, in 1989 after a similarly long conflict.

> **QUOTE >**
>
> 'What is truly worrisome about the Iran-US rivalry is how the lack of stability and communication might lead to war. And, as we've discovered in Iraq, a real war is both catastrophic for its millions of victims, and unpredictably damaging for those who start it. Lulling ourselves into thinking this is a manageable mini-Cold War… could be America's next big error of arrogance'.
>
> **John Tirman**, executive director of the US-based Center for International Studies, 'A new Cold War with Iran', *Boston Globe*, 14 August 2007.

Parallels with today?

The Cold War was relatively easy to understand. And although each side was able to destroy the other, each understood how the other behaved. It was like a huge – and deadly – version of a game where both sides know the rules.

The media often tries to describe more recent conflicts between Islamic fundamentalists and the West as a 'new Cold War'. Rightly or wrongly, they see the world as 'us and them', just as people did during the Cold War. Even military experts try to use some of the lessons learned during the Cold War to tackle terrorism and its causes. And critics of US policies see Iraq as 'another Vietnam'.

Many observers find the parallels between the photos of the Vietnam War (below) in the 1960s and those of the current US-led involvement in Iraq (left) more than superficial.

The Fundamentalist media

Christian fundamentalists (in the West, and particularly in the USA) have had more than 80 years' experience in the realm of the media, but Islamic fundamentalists have recently proved to be experts in using the Internet.

بيان تنفيذ حكم الله تعالى على المرتد المترجم من الحزب الديمقراطي الكردستاني العميل مع تحريك ذيل

بسم الله الرحمن الرحيم

A militant Iraqi group posted this image of a Kurdish man whom they later executed in 2004. His crime, according to the fundamentalists, had been to work as a translator for the US army in Iraq.

People form most of their opinions after absorbing information from different sources – newspapers and magazine, radio, television and the Internet. The collective term for all these information sources is the media, which is the plural of the word 'medium' (in this case meaning a channel or pipeline). For example, information can flow through the medium of the press (such as newspapers) or the medium of the Internet.

Most countries take pride in preserving this flow of ideas. One of the most cherished human rights is the freedom of the press, which means allowing journalists to find and report information without outside interference. Any form of control over press freedom is a form of censorship.

Two-way street

Fundamentalists understand the importance of this flow of ideas and information. Many of them, either Christians in the USA, Hindus in India or Muslims in Indonesia, believe that the world is receiving a distorted version of their message. They often accuse the media of mocking their beliefs, or at least not taking them seriously. But these fundamentalists prefer not to leave it at that – a protest and then a shrug of the shoulders. Many fundamentalists have decided to become part of the media themselves.

Fundamentalists have used the media to their advantage for more than a century. Through their newspapers, radio and television stations and websites, they have promoted 'back-to-basic' religious messages to their own congregations and beyond. In the USA,

1906 Reginal Fessendun's first successful radio broadcast (USA) contains Bible readings and hymns >>>	1922 First religious broadcast on BBC radio >>>	1931 Vatican Radio goes on air >>>	1953 Rex Humbard becomes the first 'televangelist' >>>

38

for example, Christian fundamentalists have been able to mount long-running media campaigns against abortion and the theory of evolution.

Old message, new media

America has a 200-year-old tradition of Christian preachers, or evangelists, attracting huge crowds at outdoor meetings called Revivals (because they 'revive' the original Gospel message). So it was not surprising when some of these Christian preachers took their message to the airwaves. From the late 1920s, 'radio preachers' began spreading their brand of conservative Christianity in the United States. The next step, of course, was television and since the 1950s, Americans have been able to choose from among a group of successful 'televangelists' on their screens.

Christian fundamentalists have not been alone in turning the media to their own advantage. Muslim fundamentalists also broadcast from radio and television stations within the Muslim world and beyond. And like their Christian counterparts, these Islamic fundamentalists have been quick to adapt to each new development on the Internet.

American fundamentalist Christians broadcasting on television (and known as 'televangelists') make appeals for prayers – and sometimes money – directly to viewers.

TO MAKE YOUR VOW CALL
(214) 620-6200

1961 First *Songs of Praise* programme is broadcast >>> | **2004** Islam Channel (satellite) goes on air >>> | **2006** Al-Hesbah website accused of being a message board for Muslim fundamentalists >>> | **2007** YouTubeIslam goes online >>>

39

Case Study: Danish cartoons of Muhammad

A series of 12 cartoons, some depicting the Prophet Muhammad as a terrorist, were published by the Danish newspaper *Jyllands-Posten* on 30 September 2005. The cartoons were deeply offensive to many Muslims. The fundamentalist reaction had echoes of the *Satanic Verses* affair, with the Danish paper (and its cartoonist) condemned and championed in equal measure. The cartoons led to Muslim protests in Denmark and then in many other countries. More than

Publication of the cartoons stirred many anti-Danish protests across the Muslim world.

100 people died in these protests. Meanwhile, more than 50 other newspapers chose to reprint the cartoons in support of the freedom of the press.

Contributing to the debate

Jyllands-Posten published its cartoons of Muhammad to show how difficult it is to criticise Islam. The cartoons were especially offensive to Muslims for two main reasons. The first is that Islam prohibits religious images: Muslims themselves do not have pictures of the Prophet. Secondly, the cartoons suggested that Muhammad himself would approve of bombings and other acts of terror – something that Muslims found deeply insulting.

In October 2005, 11 ambassadors from mainly Muslim countries asked the Danish prime minister for a meeting to discuss what they saw as an organised anti-Muslim campaign. The prime minister replied, saying that freedom of expression was important in Denmark. Protesters in Denmark and beyond became even angrier.

Early in 2006, Muslim protesters around the world targeted Danish, Christian and European organisations. Some protesters died – in Somalia, Afghanistan, Pakistan and other countries – when police used tough crowd-control methods. Many Muslims began a boycott of Danish goods.

Jyllands-Posten apologised for the cartoons on 31 January 2006, but the protests and reaction by some non-Muslims continued through the year before fading away.

WHAT THE WORLD THINKS...

These are three articles from newspapers around the world commenting on the Danish cartoon affair in 2006. Compare and contrast the various viewpoints and see if you can find any more newspaper reports or other media discussing the impact and aftermath of the publication of the cartoons.

Die Welt, 4 February 2006

'Islam will only become an accepted religion when there are as many jokes about Muhammad as there are about Jesus, Moses and Buddha.'

Die Welt is a German daily newspaper.

Al-Gomhuria, 2 February 2006

'It is not a question of freedom of opinion or belief, it is a conspiracy against Islam and Muslims which has been in the works for years. The international community should understand that any attack against our prophet will not go unpunished.'

Al-Gomhuria is an Egyptian newspaper published in Cairo.

The Dawn, 8 February 2006

'However, one suspects there would be a wider and more emotional response were Jesus to be disrespectfully depicted in a Muslim or a Jewish publication. And, while we're on the subject, it's probably also worth pondering whether Jyllands-Posten's efforts would have been reproduced quite so widely across Europe had the object of derision been Jews rather than Muslims.'

The Dawn is Pakistan's largest English-language newspaper.

Chapter 7

The Future of Fundamentalism

Explosion or collapse?

Religious fundamentalism show no signs of fading away, but experts cannot agree on what role it will play in world affairs in the next few decades. Christian and Islamic brands of fundamentalism have shown themselves to be powerful forces, with Christian elements now shaping some of the laws in Western countries (especially the USA). Islamic fundamentalism is even more powerful, with fundamentalists having outright control in several countries.

The question is: will these trends continue? And if not, what would stop them? These are important and complex questions and most people can only answer with educated guesses. Some people believe that fundamentalism is a temporary trend, and that people will drift away from it. Others see its influence growing and believe that fundamentalism will play an even greater role in people's lives as the message spreads further. Yet another view is that with each new terrorist act linked to Islamic fundamentalists, Christian fundamentalism will become stronger in response and that the battle lines will remain.

Test of will

Britain's most recent Prime Ministers, Tony Blair and Gordon Brown, have both spoken often about their Christian faith and how much it means to them. And although neither of these Labour party leaders could be described as a Christian fundamentalist, their pro-religion attitudes have helped them gain support from committed Christians.

On 19 December 2007, the newly elected leader of another British political party, the Liberal Democrats, expressed a dramatically different opinion. Responding to a series of questions on a national radio programme, Nick Clegg answered 'no' when asked 'do you believe in God?'. British opinion was divided about whether the response would help Clegg – because he was honest and because religion and politics should never mix – or hurt his chances among committed Christians.

About 300 women gathered at Tehran University in June 2005 to protest against gender discrimination under Iran's fundamentalist government.

A middle course?

Muslims and non-Muslims alike view Iran as a symbol of Islamic fundamentalism. Sharia dictates many of its laws, and Iran's

Lebanese Red Cross officials inspect the area around an explosion in the capital, Beirut. Lebanon has seen decades of conflict fuelled by fundamentalist groups.

most important ruler – known as the 'supreme leader' – must be a cleric. But despite automatically having a Muslim cleric in charge, Iran is also a republic and believes in democratic elections. Iranians vote for candidates to serve eight-year terms on the Assembly of Experts. This 86-member group decides on who will become the Supreme Leader. It also monitors the performance of the Leader and can replace him at any time.

The world waited expectantly as Iran went to the polls in December 2006 to elect its Assembly of Experts. Just what sort of majority would emerge – fundamentalist or otherwise – would affect how the country would be ruled. Former President Ayatollah Akbar Hashemi

Rafsanjani, a moderate, got the most votes in that election. In September 2007, Rafsanjani was elected Chairman of the Assembly of Experts. Many outside observers saw this as a signal that Iran would be more willing to find common ground with the West.

> ### QUOTE >
>
> 'You need diplomacy and not slogans. This is the place for wisdom, the place for seeking windows that will take you to the objective.'
>
> **Akbar Hashemi Rafsanjani**, former Iranian President, 'Iran Moves to Curb Hard-Liners', *Washington Post*, 8 October 2005.

1997 Sinn Fein leader Gerry Adams meets UK Prime Minister Tony Blair >>>

1998 Good Friday Agreement >>>

2007 Former arch-enemies Gerry Adams and Ian Paisley sit side by side at Stormont, seat of Northern Ireland's government >>>

Finding points in common

Despite the evident chasm between ways of thinking – and the tragic consequences of this lack of communication – fundamentalists and non-fundamentalists alike are striving to find some sort of middle ground. It is often forgotten that nearly every religious doctrine – applied fundamentally or not – calls for peace. This page and the next looks at some of the initiatives to help nurture these shared values.

The gap between Islam and the West sometimes seems to be impossible to bridge. The differences of opinion and outlook appear too far apart to find any common ground. And yet, people on both sides continue to hunt for ways to build harmony. One important route is to emphasise the importance of peace in most religions.

> **QUOTE >**
>
> '…if God had not driven some people back by means of others, monasteries, churches, synagogues and mosques, where God's name is mentioned much, would have been pulled down and destroyed. God will certainly help those who help Him – God is All-Strong, Almighty.'
>
> Koran, 22:40

Where talking has healed wounds

Recent history shows that groups can put aside their difference and find ways of working and living together. The main way forward seems to lie in being able to talk – and listen. South Africa, for example had decades of racial discrimination enshrined in its apartheid style of government. After that country's first non-racial elections, in 1994, the government set up the Truth and Reconciliation Commission (TRC). South Africans from all backgrounds began to tell their stories – asking for justice or forgiveness – helping the country to heal many of the wounds of the past.

The opponents in Northern Ireland's long-running and violent 'Troubles' eventually put aside their differences long enough to talk to each other. From the first, tense discussions in 1991 (including only some of Northern Ireland's parties), the 'peace process' gained ground. Eventually both sides saw that the whole community would benefit if they could find common ground. By late 2007, Northern Ireland was more peaceful – and more prosperous – than it had been in living memory.

Pope Benedict XVI told members of a multi-faith conference held in Rome in October 2007: 'In a world wounded by conflicts, where violence is justified in God's name, it's important to repeat that religion can never become a vehicle of hatred, it can never be used in God's name to justify violence.' Getting representatives and leaders of major religions to promote this message is an important first step.

People of the book

Fundamentalism is all about a 'back-to-basics' approach to religious belief and most fundamentalists look to sacred texts for guidance in their lives. With that in mind, many leading Muslims stress the fact that Christians and Jews are 'people of the book', the book being the Bible. All three major faiths share basic values that should lead to harmony.

Most non-Muslims, for example, are unaware that the sacred book of Islam, the Koran, explicitly praises the faithful of other denominations – Christian and Jew. And many passages from the Bible can also be interpreted as supporting all those who follow God's commandments.

The problems arise when people interpret sacred text in a narrow way, which excludes (and often threatens) those who do not share that interpretation. Many religious leaders in the forefront of promoting peace ask that their followers return to their roots. In this respect their call echoes that of the strictest fundamentalists. But the roots which these leaders refer to are the essence of their religions, sentiments such as 'do unto others as you would have others do unto you'.

Year Seven pupils, representing a range of religious and ethnic backgrounds, welcome Prime Minister Tony Blair to Mossbourne Community Academy in central London in 2005. The Academy is a new type of school, which gathers support from individuals, businesses and faith groups.

abortion Ending a pregnancy by removing an unborn baby.

abstain Choose not to do something.

adherence Strict obedience to customs, rules and regulations.

al Qaeda A fundamentalist Muslim military organisation, responsible for the 9/11 attacks and other acts of terrorism.

apartheid A form of government in South Africa from 1948 to 1990 which gave full rights only to white citizens.

bin Laden, Osama A Saudi Arabian fundamentalist Muslim (born 1957), founder of al Qaeda.

blasphemous Making fun of, or insulting, God.

boycott A decision not to do business, or have any contact with, an individual or group as a form of protest.

Buddhism One of the world's major religions, founded in India in the 6th century BCE.

caliphate a large area governed by a Muslim ruler.

Catholic A member of the Catholic church, based in Rome and acknowledging its leader (the Pope) as God's representative on Earth. The term Roman Catholic is sometimes used, to acknowledge the church's headquarters in Rome.

censorship Controlling what can and cannot be said or written by the media.

Christian Someone who follows the teaching of Jesus Christ.

cleric An official in an organised religion.

coalition A group of individuals or countries working together for a common cause.

Cold War A tense period following the end of World War II which saw the USA and its allies and the USSR and its allies constantly on the alert for war against the other side.

conservative Preferring a return to older, simpler ways.

constitution A written document stating how an organisation or government can operate.

Crusades A series of invasions by European Christians aimed at capturing parts of the Holy Land that were under Muslim control.

discrimination Unfair treatment because of religion, political views, sexuality, disability, appearance, etc.

embassy A government office based in a foreign country but representing the home country.

evolution Relating to a scientific theory that all living things change over time and that these changes are passed on to new generations.

exile A period of time (voluntary or enforced) away from one's own country.

extradite To send someone back to a country where he or she is suspected of committing a crime.

Holy Land The areas described in the Bible; sometimes described as the Promised Land as many people believe that God promised it to the Jews in biblical times.

heretic Someone who calls for changes to an accepted belief, especially in religion.

inerrancy Being without any form of error or mistake.

Islamism A belief that Islam is not only a religion but a political system

Khomeini, Ayatollah Ruhollah The spiritual (and sometimes political) leader of Iran from the fall of the Shah until his death in 1989.

Koran The sacred book of Islam, which believes that it was revealed to the Prophet Muhammad by the angel Gabriel.

media The collective name for information-gathering organizations such as newspapers, television, radio and the Internet

Modern Era A loose description of the historical period from the end of the 18th century to the present.

Muhammad An Arab merchant who founded the Islamic faith after revealing the teachings of the Koran to followers.

Mujahideen A term to describe Muslims engaged in a holy war; it is often used to describe Muslims who fought to remove Russian influence from Afghanistan in the 1980s.

Muslim Brotherhood The largest Islamist organisation in the world, which promotes the interests of Islam internationally.

NATO An abbreviation of the North Atlantic Treaty Organisation, a military alliance of 26 countries.

9/11 attacks A series of attacks on US cities by Islamic terrorists on 11 September 2001.

Old Testament The books of the Bible that were written before the time of Jesus Christ.

Orthodox Christian A Christian who follows the Greek or Russian traditions of worship, customs and language. Orthodox Christians form the third main Christian branch, along with Catholics and Protestants.

Ottoman Empire A Turkish-controlled empire which controlled much of the Middle East and some of Eastern Europe from 1299 to 1923.

Protestant A follower of one of the Christian denominations that split from the Catholic church at the time of the Reformation.

Orthodox Jews Jews who believe in a very strict interpretation of their sacred books.

peer A member of the House of Lords, the upper (unelected) house of the British Parliament.

Reformation A period in the early 16th century when Christian protesters (later called Protestants) left the Catholic Church.

refugee Someone who has been driven from his or her home by war or disaster.

Shah The term to describe a former hereditary ruler of Iran.

Sharia Islamic law based on the Koran (Islam's sacred book).

Taliban Islamic fundamentalists who ruled Afghanistan from 1996 to 2001.

tenet A central belief (for example, of a religion).

Thirty Years War A conflict (1618–48) involving most European powers and centring on Catholic-Protestant tensions

War on Terror A series of US-led actions around the world, beginning in the aftermath of the 9/11 attacks and intended to reduce terrorism worldwide

weapons of mass destruction Biological or chemical weapons that can kill or injure people in a large area.

West A loose term to describe countries, mainly in Europe and North America, that never had a large Muslim population.

West Bank A region along the western bank of the River Jordan, which Israel has claimed since 1967; Palestinians and other Arabs dispute this claim.

World War II WWII was a global conflict (1939–45) in which the UK, USA, USSR and their allies defeated Germany, Japan and their allies.

Index

FURTHER INFORMATION >

BOOKS

Fundamentalism (Ideas of the Modern World)
by Alex Woolf (Hodder Children's Books, 2003)

Islam (Opposing Voices)
by Jennifer A. Hurley (Greenhaven, 2001)

Islamic Fundamentalism
by Kim Whitehead (Mason Crest, 2006)

Religious Extremes
by Otto James (Smart Apple Media, 2006)

The Rise of Islamic Fundamentalism
edited by Philip Marquilies (Greenhaven, 2005)

WEBSITES

Arabia: The Wahhabi Movement
http://www.naqshbandi.org/ottomans/wahhabi/origins.htm
Description of the fundamentalist Wahhabi movement, originating in Saudi Arabia.

Fundamentalism and Faith
http://www.bbc.co.uk/worldservice/programmes/archive/020917_fundamentalism.shtml
Archive broadcasts and transcripts from the BBC World Service series on fundamentalism.

Islam in America
http://www.americanmuslims.info/
The website of the Council on American-Islamic Relations (CAIR).

The Muslim Brotherhood
http://www.ikhwanweb.com
The Muslim Brotherhood website has wide-ranging information about the organisation.

Why They Hate Us
http://www.nationalreview.com/comment/comment-takeyh100901.shtml
A conservative American's attempt to make sense of 9/11 and Islamic fundamentalism.